JB DIANA
O'Shei, Tim.
Diana, Princess of Wales /
by Tim O'Shei.

Snap books™

Queens and Princesses

FOUNTAINDALE PUBLIC LIBRARY DISTRICT
300 West Briarcliff Road
Bolingbrook, IL 60440-2894
(630) 759-2102

Diana
PRINCESS OF WALES

by Tim O'Shei

Consultant:

Glenn A. Steinberg, PhD

Associate Professor of English

The College of New Jersey

Ewing, New Jersey

Capstone
press®

Mankato, Minnesota

Snap Books are published by Capstone Press,
151 Good Counsel Drive, P.O. Box 669, Mankato, Minnesota 56002.
www.capstonepress.com

Copyright © 2009 by Capstone Press, a Capstone Publishers company.
All rights reserved. No part of this publication may be reproduced
in whole or in part, or stored in a retrieval system, or transmitted in any form or by
any means, electronic, mechanical, photocopying, recording, or otherwise, without
written permission of the publisher.
For information regarding permission, write to Capstone Press,
151 Good Counsel Drive, P.O. Box 669, Dept. R, Mankato, Minnesota 56002.
Printed in the United States of America

Library of Congress Cataloging-in-Publication Data
O'Shei, Tim.
    Diana, Princess of Wales / by Tim O'Shei.
    p. cm. — (Snap books. Queens and princesses)
    Summary: "Describes the life and death of Diana, Princess of Wales" —
Provided by publisher.
    Includes bibliographical references and index.
    ISBN-13: 978-1-4296-1954-7 (hardcover)
    ISBN-10: 1-4296-1954-6 (hardcover)
    1. Diana, Princess of Wales, 1961–1997 — Juvenile literature. 2. Princesses —
Great Britain — Biography — Juvenile literature. I. Title. II. Series.
DA591.A45D5354 2009
941.085092 — dc22   2008000628

Editor: Christine Peterson
Designer: Juliette Peters
Photo Researcher: Wanda Winch

Photo Credits:
AP Images/Press Association, 23; Corbis/Hulton-Deutsch Collection, 19; Corbis/
Quadrillion, 6; Getty Images Inc./Hulton Archive/Fox Photos, 7; Getty Images Inc./
Lichfield Archive, 5, 8; Getty Images Inc./Tim Graham, 17, 20, 21, 25, 26, cover;
Getty Images Inc./WireImage/Anwar Hussein, 13, 16, 28, 29; iStockphoto/Mary Lane,
17; Landov LLC/Alpha, 12; Landov LLC/Maxppp/J.L. Macault, 27; Landov LLC/PA
Photos, 11; Landov LLC/Reuters/Vanderlei Almeida, 22; SuperStock Inc./SuperStock,
9, 15

Essential content terms are **bold** and are defined at the bottom of the page where
they first appear.

1 2 3 4 5 6 13 12 11 10 09 08

Table of Contents

A ROYAL
Bride

Lady Diana Spencer didn't look like a woman who was about to become a princess. She was sitting in jeans, staring at the TV while an assistant worked on her short blonde hair. The day was July 29, 1981, and the news featured endless stories about Diana. In just a few hours, 20-year-old Diana would marry Prince Charles. He was heir to the British throne.

Most of the world's attention was focused on London, England, and the royal wedding. Just thinking about all the attention made Diana nervous.

TWO TIARAS

The day before the wedding, Prince Charles' mother, Queen Elizabeth II, gave Diana a red leather box. Diana opened the box and pulled out a stunning tiara. Called the Lover's Knot, it had 19 diamond arches, each holding a pearl. It had belonged to the queen's family for nearly 70 years.

Lady Diana Spencer grabbed the world's attention when she married Prince Charles on July 29, 1981.

But Diana chose to wear the Spencer family tiara for her wedding. Made in 1830, this tiara featured hundreds of diamonds set in scrolls, tulips, and star-shaped flowers. As Diana watched TV, a royal helper carefully pinned it into her hair.

Soon after, Diana stepped into her wedding dress. The ivory gown was made from six different fabrics. The gown's 25-foot (8-meter) train was the longest in royal wedding history. Stylists then pinned a veil to the tiara. The veil was made from 150 yards (137 meters) of ivory netting. It was as long as the gown's train.

Diana was worried that she would get tangled or trip in the gown. To prepare for her wedding, Diana had practiced walking around a ballroom dragging two bed sheets tied together. Now she took her first steps as a royal bride.

Diana worried about getting tangled in the record-setting train of her wedding gown.

WEDDING GLAMOUR

Newspapers called the event the "wedding of the century." It was one of the most expensive royal weddings ever held. It all started with the engagement ring. Diana chose a blue sapphire the size of a man's knuckle. The huge jewel was surrounded by 14 diamonds. The gems were mounted on a white-gold ring. The ring cost $63,000. In 1981, that was enough money to buy nine cars.

Diana asked British designers Elizabeth and David Emanuel to create her gown. Diana's dress was made of 25 yards (23 meters) of silk produced by the silkworms at a royal farm. The gown featured wide puffed sleeves. Layers of lace ruffles were gathered around the neck, sleeves, and skirt. It was decorated with 10,000 pearls. A small gold-and-diamond horseshoe was attached to the waist for good luck. Diana's gown soon became one of the most copied wedding dresses in history.

FAIRY-TALE CEREMONY

Later that morning, soldiers lined the London streets as horses pulled Diana's glass carriage to St. Paul's Cathedral. Behind the soldiers, 1 million cheering people packed the streets.

Five bridesmaids started up the aisle. Dressed in ivory taffeta, the bridesmaids ranged in age from 11 to just 5 years old. The crowd stood as Diana's father walked her up the aisle, which was longer than a football field. The young bride smiled as she walked toward the altar carrying a huge bouquet of roses, gardenias, and lilies. Diana's ivory silk wedding shoes, covered with 150 pearls, peeked out beneath the dress as she walked.

Diana made sure her five young bridesmaids were ready to walk up the aisle.

Crowds cheered when the royal newlyweds kissed on the balcony of Buckingham Palace.

Both Charles and Diana were nervous during the 75-minute ceremony. The church was packed with more than 3,500 guests, including royalty and world leaders. At least 750 million people watched the ceremony on TV. When it was over, Lady Diana Spencer became the Princess of Wales.

After the ceremony, the royal couple rode to Buckingham Palace in an open carriage. The British people cheered the royal couple. Crowds gathered outside Buckingham Palace, and started chanting, "We want Di!" Standing on the palace balcony, the newlyweds kissed. The crowd roared. The cameras clicked away. From that day on, the cameras and crowds never stopped focusing on Princess Diana.

2

A NOBLE

Girl

Lady Diana Frances Spencer was, in her words, "supposed to be a boy." She was born on July 1, 1961, in Sandringham, England, to wealthy English **nobles**, Edward "Johnnie" and Frances Spencer. The Spencers were distant relatives of the royal family. Diana's grandfather was the 7th Earl Spencer. When he died, Diana's father became the 8th Earl Spencer and received the family fortune. Johnnie Spencer needed a son to carry on the family name and title. He and Frances had two daughters, Sarah, 6, and Jane, 4. Diana was the third. They loved her, but they had hoped for a son.

WEALTHY BUT UNHAPPY

Diana spent her first years living in Park House, a 10-bedroom mansion on a royal estate. She loved to be with her older sisters and to play mother to her dolls. In 1964, Diana's parents finally had a son, Charles. Diana dressed and cared for her younger brother like one of her dolls.

Even at age 1, Diana enjoyed spending time outdoors.

noble — an upper-class person of high rank

As she grew older, Diana loved caring for animals. She had many pets, including guinea pigs, hamsters, and rabbits. Her favorite pet was a cat named Marmalade. For her 7th birthday, her father hired a local zookeeper to bring a camel called Bert. Diana and 20 children rode Bert around the Park House lawn.

Diana's favorite activity was dancing. She started taking lessons at age 3 and dreamed of becoming a ballerina. Diana trained both in and out of school. But her dream ended when she grew too tall.

Although Diana's family enjoyed a comfortable life, her parents weren't getting along. When Diana was 6, her parents divorced. Diana was hurt and confused. After the divorce, Diana split her time between her father's estate and her mother's home. Diana never felt fully loved or at home.

NOBLES AND ROYALTY

Althorp, the Spencer family estate

Members of the royal family are direct relatives of the monarch. A noble family has a connection with a king or queen. Usually, a noble family's ancestor represented the royal family hundreds of years ago in the military or in another land. They may have also done a special service for the ruler. In thanks, the monarch gave the ancestor land, riches, and a title. The title and wealth is passed from one generation to the next.

Sometimes, like with the Spencers, the family is distantly related to the royal family. But nobles will never become king or queen, unless they marry a monarch.

DIANA'S PRINCE

As a teenager, Diana was a natural athlete. She did well in sports like tennis, swimming, diving, and field hockey. However, she struggled in school. Instead of college, she attended a finishing school in Switzerland. In 1978, Diana returned to England and spent a few months as a nanny. She then moved to London where she shared an apartment with friends. Diana wanted to pay her own bills and not depend on her parents' money. She took jobs as a house cleaner, waitress, and kindergarten teacher.

When Diana was 16, her older sister Sarah introduced her to Prince Charles. He was the oldest son of Queen Elizabeth II and next in line for the British throne. The prince was also 13 years older than Diana. During the next few years, Diana and Prince Charles saw each other at parties and other social events. Slowly, the friendship became a romance. By the time Diana was 19, she was dating the prince. The relationship changed her life forever.

Diana took pride in her work as a kindergarten teacher in London.

finishing school — a private school for girls that prepares them for social activities

3

ROYAL *Celebrity*

Diana and the prince tried to keep their relationship a secret, but it didn't work. Photographers and reporters followed Charles everywhere he went. Now they followed Diana too. Anytime Diana left her apartment, cameras clicked away.

The prince seemed to be seriously interested in Diana. The British people were interested too. If Charles married her, Diana could one day become queen.

The media attention made Diana miserable. "Everywhere I go, there's someone there," she said. "If I go to a restaurant or just out shopping to the supermarket, they're trying to take photographs."

The press nicknamed Diana "Shy Di." Reporters pestered her with questions. The press, British people, and royal watchers around the world all had the same questions. Did Diana love the prince? Would she marry him? Diana didn't answer those questions in public. But if Charles asked her these questions, she knew what her answer would be.

Charles and Diana announced their engagement on February 24, 1981, at Buckingham Palace in London.

CHOOSING A QUEEN

For Prince Charles, marriage was an historic event. He wasn't just choosing a wife. He was choosing a future queen. When Charles proposed to Diana, he explained what marrying into the royal family would mean to her. He told Diana that her life would change forever. Her privacy would vanish. Prince Charles told Diana to think about it carefully. He gave her several days to give him her answer. But Diana knew right away. Her answer was yes.

Their engagement was announced in February 1981. Five months later, Britain had a new princess. Diana and Charles honeymooned on the Mediterranean Sea aboard a yacht called the *Britannia*. Afterward, they spent a few months at Balmoral, the royal family's home in Scotland.

After their honeymoon, Charles and Diana relaxed at the royal family's home in Scotland.

LIFE OF LUXURY

As Charles promised, Diana's life became very different. One of Diana's first royal duties was to build up her wardrobe. As a princess, she needed fashionable clothes. Editors from the fashion magazine *Vogue* helped Diana choose clothes. They also taught her how to walk and pose for cameras.

Diana and Charles spent most of their time in two homes. One was a country home called Highgrove. This estate sits on 350 acres (142 hectares) of land and has a farm next door. It has nine bedrooms and six bathrooms. In London, the couple lived in Kensington Palace, a 25-room mansion divided into apartments.

At home, Diana had servants to look after her needs. She had a private secretary, cooks, butlers, and drivers. As a princess, Diana couldn't travel anywhere alone. Bodyguards followed her everywhere. Being a princess brought Diana fame and wealth, but it took away much of her freedom.

Diana kept track of her royal duties in her office at Kensington Palace (at right).

4

THE PEOPLE'S
Princess

Diana didn't fit in well with the rest of the royal family. They were stiff and serious in public. Diana was warm and friendly. She wanted to be close to people. In public, Diana would hug people and shake their hands. The British people adored her. When Diana and Charles appeared in public, people cheered louder for her. They reached out to shake her hand. They gave her piles of flowers. Prince Charles always smiled when this happened, but he also found it frustrating.

A MOTHER FOR TWO

Diana loved children and wanted to be a mother. Ten months after their wedding, Charles and Diana's first son, William, was born. After his father, William is next in line to become king. His birth on June 21, 1982, was celebrated with a 41-gun salute in London. On September 15, 1984, the couple's second son, Harry, was born.

Everywhere Diana went, she was greeted by crowds of cheering people.

Royal children receive special treatment. They attend the best schools and dress in the finest clothes. They learn traditional sports, including horseback riding, polo, skiing, and hunting. But Diana wanted William and Harry to learn more about life. She wanted her sons to experience the same fun as regular kids. Diana often took them on trips to beaches and amusement parks. One day, guests at Disney World in Florida received a royal surprise. Crowds watched as Diana and the young princes roared down Splash Mountain.

Diana and Charles spent time with Harry, left, and William, right, at the family's Highgrove estate.

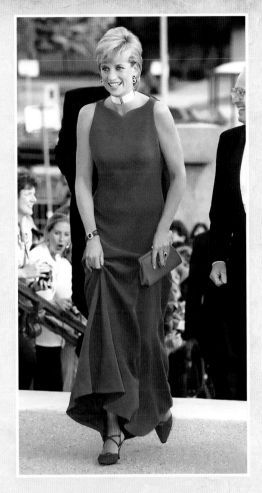

ROYAL STYLE

Diana was one of the world's most fashionable women.
People watched and often copied her style. It started with her
hair. Diana got a short, stylish cut for her wedding to Prince
Charles. Soon women around the world copied the "Di Cut."

To help with her royal wardrobe, Diana often turned to
famous fashion designers. Her favorite designer was Catherine
Walker. This London designer created many of Diana's most
memorable gowns. The princess also wore original designs by
Versace, Valentino, and Chanel.

The princess wore many styles of clothes. She was well
known for elegant formal gowns. But Diana also caught people's
attention in stylish business suits. She wore bold designs, such
as plaids, stripes, and even polka dots. Diana also loved hats.
During six months in 1985, she wore 27 different hats.

Diana wanted her sons to understand that other people were not as well off as they were. As the boys grew older, she took them to visit villages, hospitals, and other places where people were struggling.

Everywhere Princess Diana went, cameras followed. Diana used this extra attention to help charities. She raised money for breast cancer, AIDS research, and other causes. Diana visited hospital patients of all ages. She sat and talked with patients, rather than just posing for photos. In 1984, Diana made headlines when she hugged an **AIDS** patient. At that time, people were just learning about the disease. They were often afraid to touch people with AIDS. Diana helped change that.

Diana often reached out to shake hands or hug people with AIDS and other illnesses.

AIDS — an illness in which the body's ability to protect itself against disease is destroyed

By the 1990s, Charles and Diana's marriage had become tense and unhappy.

UNHAPPY MARRIAGE

Diana won the hearts of the British people, but privately she was unhappy. She developed an eating disorder called **bulimia**. Her marriage was crumbling. The couple had different interests and spent much of their time apart. In 1992, Charles and Diana separated. They divorced in 1996.

"I'd like to be a queen of people's hearts."

From a British TV interview with Princess Diana, November 1995

bulimia — an eating disorder in which a person overeats and then purposely vomits the food

'IS SHE AN *Angel?*'

After her divorce, Princess Diana was no longer known as Her Royal Highness. However, she kept her title as Princess of Wales. The press and public remained fascinated with the newly single Diana. The paparazzi still followed her every move.

Diana seemed happy to be on her own and work for causes she believed in. The princess still wanted to use her fame to help others. At her son William's suggestion, Diana decided to use her huge wardrobe to benefit charities. She had dozens of expensive gowns hanging in her closet. Each morning for a month, Diana looked through her closet. She finally chose 70 gowns to sell for charity. In 1997, Diana's gowns were sold at an auction in New York City. The event raised $5.7 million for AIDS and cancer work. One dark-blue velvet gown sold for $222,500. In 1985, Diana had worn it to the White House where she danced with actor John Travolta.

In 1997, Diana sold 70 of her gowns and raised $5.7 million for charity.

paparazzi — aggressive photographers who take pictures of celebrities to sell to magazines or newspapers

CHAMPIONING A CAUSE

In 1997, the cameras followed Diana to some of the most dangerous places in the world. She spent time in Africa and Bosnia-Herzegovina, where wars had torn apart lives. In these areas, land mines had been used as weapons during the wars. Some of the deadly explosives remained buried years after the wars had ended. Diana knew she could bring attention to this problem. She risked her safety walking through areas littered with land mines. She met with people who had lost legs and arms to explosions. In one hospital, Diana met a 7-year-old girl named Helena. The girl was dying from injuries she received in a land mine blast. Diana spoke to Helena and rubbed her hand. When Diana left, Helena asked, "Is she an angel?"

Diana wore protective body armor as she visited a field being cleared of land mines in Angola.

"I no longer want to live someone else's idea of what and who I should be. I am going to be me."

Princess Diana, from an interview with biographer Andrew Morton, as published in *Diana: Her True Story*

LOVE AND TRAGEDY

That year, Diana began dating wealthy businessman Dodi Fayed. They dined in fine restaurants. They vacationed on private yachts and on sunny islands. Everywhere the couple went, a pack of photographers followed.

On Saturday evening, August 30, 1997, Diana and Dodi were dining at the Ritz-Carlton hotel in Paris, France. Crowds of photographers waited outside the hotel hoping to snap a photo of the couple. Shortly after midnight, Diana and Dodi slipped out of the hotel and into their car. The couple hoped to escape to Dodi's apartment.

During the summer of 1997, Diana began a relationship with businessman Dodi Fayed.

A black Mercedes sped away from the hotel. Seated inside the luxury car were the couple, a bodyguard, and the driver. A pack of paparazzi pursued the car. The driver sped up. So did the photographers. As the car headed into a tunnel, it crashed into a concrete wall. The crash instantly killed Dodi and the driver, Henri Paul. Diana and the bodyguard, Trevor Rees-Jones, were pulled from the wreck. Rees-Jones was badly injured but survived. Diana was brought to a hospital, but her injuries were too severe. She died early Sunday morning, August 31, 1997.

PRINCESS OF HEARTS

People around the world mourned Diana. In London, people left a sea of flower bouquets and gifts outside her home. Millions of people lined the streets to watch her funeral procession. Millions more watched the funeral on TV. Diana was buried on a small, private island on her family's Althorp estate.

Charles, William (right), and Harry (center) look over the countless flowers and cards left in memory of Diana.

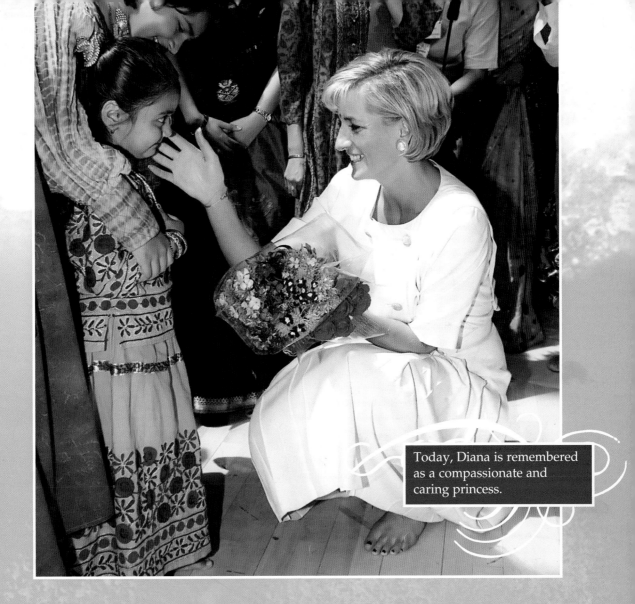

Today, Diana is remembered as a compassionate and caring princess.

Today, people remember Diana for her warm smile, caring nature, and tireless work for charities. She used her fame to win attention for issues that were often ignored. But Diana was also a mother who passed on her sense of caring to her sons. Today, both William and Harry volunteer with many charities. In 2007, they honored Diana by organizing a concert in her memory. The event was broadcast throughout the world and raised more than $2 million for charity.

Diana became a princess for the ordinary people. She brought new life to the role of royalty in Great Britain. Shy Lady Diana Spencer changed what it means to be a princess today.

Glossary

AIDS (AYDZ) — an illness in which the body's ability to protect itself against disease is destroyed

ancestor (AN-ses-tuhr) — a member of a person's family who lived a long time ago

bulimia (buh-LEE-mee-uh) — an eating disorder in which a person overeats and then purposely vomits the food

divorce (di-VORSS) — the ending of a marriage by a court of law

estate (e-STAYT) — a large area of land, usually with a house on it

finishing school (FIN-ish-ing SKOOL) — a private school for girls where students are prepared for social activities

heir (AIR) — someone who has been or will be left a title, property, or money

land mine (LAND MINE) — a bomb buried underground

monarch (MON-urk) — a ruler, such as a king or queen, who often inherits his or her position

mourn (MORN) — to be very sad and miss someone who has died

noble (NOH-buhl) — an upper-class person of high rank

paparazzi (pah-puh-RAHT-see) — aggressive photographers who take pictures of celebrities to sell to magazines or newspapers

tiara (tee-AR-uh) — a piece of jewelry that looks like a small crown

Read More

Gormley, Beatrice. *Diana, Princess of Wales: Young Royalty.* Childhood of World Figures. New York: Aladdin Paperbacks, 2005.

Mattern, Joanne. *Princess Diana.* DK Biography. New York: DK Publishing, 2006.

Powell, Jillian. *Looking at Great Britain.* Looking at Countries. Milwaukee: Gareth Stevens, 2008.

Internet Sites

FactHound offers a safe, fun way to find Internet sites related to this book. All of the sites on FactHound have been researched by our staff.

Here's how:

1. Visit *www.facthound.com*
2. Choose your grade level.
3. Type in this book ID **1429619546** for age-appropriate sites. You may also browse subjects by clicking on letters, or by clicking on pictures and words.
4. Click on the **Fetch It** button.

FactHound will fetch the best sites for you!

Index